D
IN
PAST

Shirley Kay

Illustrated by Mark Peppé

Explorer 12   Puffin Books

Acknowledgements

The author and publishers would like to thank the following for their
kind permission to reproduce the photographs appearing in this book:

Ashmolean Museum, Oxford, pp. 31 and 33; Peter Clayton, pp. 7, 8 and 32;
Hirmer Verlag, Munich, p. 17; Jericho Excavation Fund, p. 40;
Metropolitan Museum of Art, New York, p. 29; Middle East Archive, p. 21;
the Radio Times Hulton Picture Library, pp. 6, 10 and 22; the Trustees of
the British Museum, pp. 15, 17, 24, 28, 36 and 37; UNESCO, Paris, p. 45.

The illustration on the title page is a detail from
The Standard of Ur, early Dynasty II.

PUFFIN BOOKS:
A Division of Penguin Books Ltd
Harmondsworth, Middlesex, England
Penguin Books Inc., 7110 Ambassador Road,
Baltimore, Maryland 21207, U.S.A.
Penguin Books Australia Ltd, Ringwood,
Victoria, Australia

First published 1974

Made and printed in Great Britain by
Westerham Press Ltd, Westerham, Kent
Set in Monophoto Optima

Introduction

In ancient times men hunted and fished and gathered wild grain for their food. They had no permanent homes and travelled about for thousands of years in order to find enough to eat. But about eleven or twelve thousand years ago, some groups of people discovered that they could plant grain themselves and collect it when it ripened. This was the beginning of agriculture and it meant that they had to stay in one place while their grain was growing. So they began to build houses.

Gradually a collection of houses grew into a village and then a town, with a temple, and fortresses to protect them. Life became more complicated and the people elected kings to rule them and invented writing to communicate with one another. They could afford and enjoy art and sculpture and jewellery. They built great buildings, created beautiful things and wrote books. We call this kind of life *civilization*.

Civilization as we know it began in the Middle East more than 5,000 years ago. It is very hot and dry there and crops grow quickly where rivers bring water. It was there, beside those rivers, that the first towns were built and the first kingdoms developed.

Along the banks of the Nile River, the ancient Egyptians developed their civilization. It lasted for about 3,000 years (half as long again as the time from Jesus Christ until today). The ruins of their massive temples, pyramids and tombs still stand beside the Nile, decorated with the pictures and signs of their hieroglyphic writing.

About the same time and a thousand miles away, in the valley of the Tigris and Euphrates rivers, in the land now called Iraq, a series of ancient kingdoms rose and flourished and conquered their neighbours. Then, in their turn, they were conquered, and all that remains are the large, steep mounds of earth which covered the ruins of their towns, built one on top of the other until hills were formed. Buried in those ruins were the beautiful objects they had made and libraries full of their stories, history and learning.

Ever since the Middle Ages, adventurous Europeans have visited the Middle East and brought back tales of strange ruins, but until recently little was known about them or the people who had built them.

• Bogazköy

• Hacilar

TURKEY

MEDITERRANEAN SEA

• Jerusalem

Jericho •

□ Cairo

Giza ⊞

Saqqara •

EGYPT

River Nile

• Tell el Amarna

Abydos •

• Naqada

Thebes

RED SEA

• Abu Simbel

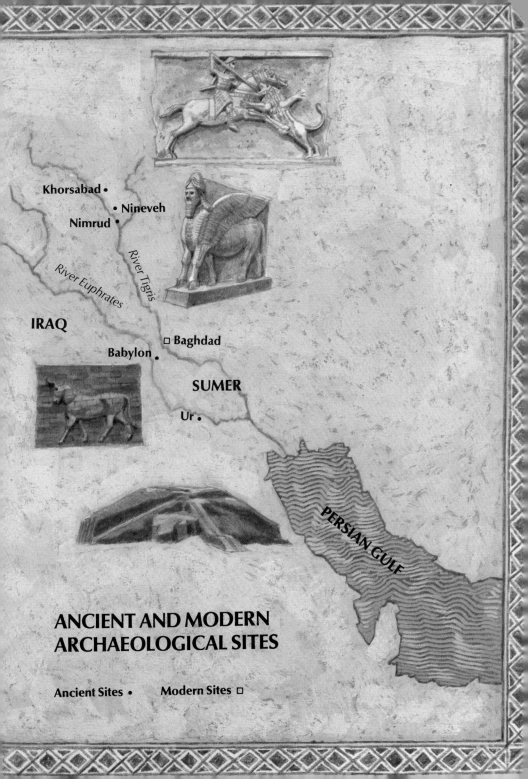

Khorsabad •

• Nineveh

Nimrud •

River Euphrates

River Tigris

IRAQ

□ Baghdad

Babylon •

SUMER

Ur •

PERSIAN GULF

ANCIENT AND MODERN
ARCHAEOLOGICAL SITES

Ancient Sites •   Modern Sites □

Gradually people in Europe became more curious about the civilizations of the past. When the French leader, Napoleon, invaded Egypt in 1798 he took a team of scholars with him, to study the ruins. These scholars wrote about all they found there and this encouraged many other Europeans to go and explore the ruins.

At first most of them merely wanted to collect all the ancient objects they could find, to take back to their own countries. But intelligent people soon realized that it was more important, and more interesting, to try to learn about the past than to fill boxes full of ancient statues and vases. And so they began to excavate (dig) carefully, to write about all they found, and to compare it with things others had found.

In this way archaeology – or the study of the past – began. During the last hundred years or so archaeologists have managed to piece together much of the history of the great civilizations of the ancient Middle East. They are still working there today, finding out a little more each year.

But this book is mainly about some of the archaeologists who have unearthed the ruins of the Middle East during the past 150 years, the methods they have used, and what they have discovered.

A Collector's Paradise in Egypt

The giant head moved, inch by inch, across the desert on its wooden sledge, slipping over tree-trunk rollers. In the hot mid-summer of 1816 it must have seemed an odd sight to the Egyptians of Thebes, once the capital of ancient Egypt but now a ruin, to see the giant head on the move. And no doubt the foreigner, Giovanni Belzoni, who was moving

the head, seemed odder still. He was a giant of a man, six feet six inches (2·1 m) tall and immensely strong. He was the son of a poor Italian barber and had gone to London to be the strong man in a circus. While there he became interested in arranging water shows, and he came to Egypt to sell a water wheel which he had invented. The sale fell through, and the only way he could see to make a living was to use his strength collecting ancient objects.

Belzoni and his men moving the giant Head

These ancient objects – statues, vases and jewellery – were becoming so popular in Europe that the English and French consuls in Egypt were sending out agents to hunt for them everywhere. The methods they used were very rough and they did not care how much damage they did to the ancient buildings they robbed, or to each other – for at times they came to blows. They took everything they could move, and in those days the local authorities were not interested in ancient things. They did not stop the collectors; indeed, they were quite willing to give them permission to carry away what they fancied – for a small fee.

Belzoni was a treasure-hunter like the other Europeans, but he was more successful because he was immensely strong, hard working and determined. He was ingenious too, and clever at thinking out ways of doing things. The giant head that he moved had not escaped the notice of the French some years earlier: it was very beautiful but it weighed seven or eight tonnes. The French had bored a hole in its shoulder, to blow off the lower part with dynamite, or else to fix a rope to it, but they gave up. Belzoni, who was penniless, had to succeed in moving it or starve. He persevered despite the heat which made him ill, and finally brought the head to the river Nile, from where it could be taken by boat all the way to London. It now stands in the British Museum, the hole still in its shoulder. Belzoni did not know whose head it was. Nobody did in those days. Now we know it was the head of a great conqueror, the Pharaoh Ramesses II, who ruled Egypt for nearly seventy years, from 1304 to 1237 B.C. Belzoni was soon to meet this face again.

The explorer friend who had told him of the head also told him of a cliff in the south of Egypt where there was a splendid temple with huge statues. Near that temple he had noticed the tips of even bigger statues, sticking out of the sand. Belzoni set off by boat up the river Nile and came to the place called Abu Simbel. He saw the tips of colossal statues; the head of one of them stood just above the sand, and it was taller than Belzoni himself, its ear alone was three feet six inches (1·1m) high. It had the same face as the giant head he had moved.

Belzoni was sure that there must be a temple carved in the cliff here, but he calculated that the doorway must be beneath thirty-five feet (10·6 m) of sand, sand so soft and dry that digging through it would be like trying 'to make a hole in water'. He felt quite disheartened, but was very determined, so he asked the local sheikh for workmen.

There were no special tools for archaeological work in those days, so the workmen brought along a tool they used in their own fields – a kind of solid rake. Two ropes were attached to it so that two men could work it, pulling it back by the handle then the other pulling it forward by the ropes. As they cleared the sand away Belzoni put up fences of palm branches to try and stop the sand from sliding back into the hole.

Progress was very slow and the workmen gave up in disgust, so Belzoni and five of his friends finished the job alone. They were the first men for hundreds of years to enter the magnificent temple inside the cliff. They found themselves in a great hall with statues carved from floor to ceiling, and scenes of the Pharaoh's battles carved and painted on the walls. It was the greatest temple in southern Egypt, but for Belzoni it was rather a disappointment because there was almost nothing he could move, and therefore nothing he could sell.

He then decided to concentrate on tombs, which might provide richer pickings. The Arabs who had helped him move the giant head at Thebes were experienced tomb robbers, and they took him into some of the tombs they had found in western Thebes, underground passages full of the bodies of ancient Egyptians ('stacked like macaroni cheese' as another Italian had once described them). These bodies called *mummies* had been preserved and wrapped in linen bandages. Wrapped among the bandages were rolls of papyrus with writings on them, and some-times jewellery, and tomb robbers broke up the mummies to find these valuable objects. Belzoni found that even as he crawled through the dark, hot, stuffy passages the fragile mummies crunched to pieces.

The tomb robbers knew that in the bleak rocky valley near by, called the Valley of the Kings, there were still hidden some of the secret tombs of the ancient Pharaohs. But they had not been able to find them. Belzoni decided he would try, in the hope of finding great treasures there which would make him rich. He walked all over the valley wondering where to begin. At last he noticed that in some places the earth and stones were less tightly packed than in others. He decided to dig in these places and each time he found an ancient royal tomb. But all of them had been robbed long ago.

Finally he tried a place where a stream ran after rain. His Arab friends told him it was a crazy place to dig, but again he was right. This time he found a magnificent underground tomb – the tomb of Seti I, father of Ramesses II. Again it had been robbed: the rope used by the tomb robbers of the past still hung there, so old that it crumbled to dust as Belzoni touched it. But the beautiful carved alabaster coffin was still there, and over a thousand painted or carved figures still decorated the walls. Belzoni made a model of the tomb which he exhibited in London and it made him famous.

It also taught him another lesson of archaeology. 'Finding the tomb,' he wrote, 'has given me that satisfaction, that extreme pleasure which wealth cannot purchase; the pleasure of discovering what has long been sought in vain.' He experienced that pleasure once again when in 1818 he visited the pyramids of Giza. Those massive tombs of the kings of ancient Egypt were still a puzzle; although the largest of them was open, the others appeared to have no entrances at all.

Belzoni walked all round the second pyramid and determined to find the way in. Suddenly he again saw looser earth on the north side, and he dug there although people laughed at him. He was right: the ground had been disturbed, but only by robbers in ancient times. He studied the largest pyramid again for a whole day – just looking and thinking. He found that the entrance was not exactly in the middle of the north side, as everyone had supposed, but slightly to the east of centre, and so it was

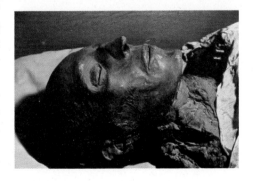

Mummified head of Seti I

possible that the entrance to the second pyramid would also be in the same position. This time, when he prised out some of the massive stones of the pyramid, he found the true entrance behind them, but the burial chamber was empty, robbed long ago.

Belzoni solved the puzzle of the pyramid by observation, patience and thought, as modern archaeologists would try to do. But for many years after him other excavators still resorted to dynamite to find the way into the pyramids.

Archaeological Discovery in the Middle East

The Mounds of Assyria

A thousand miles (1,610 km) away to the east of Egypt, other ancient kingdoms had flourished beside the Tigris and Euphrates rivers. One of these kingdoms was that of the Assyrians, the terror of the ancient world. Their armies constantly attacked the people to the north, south, east and west of them. They even invaded Egypt. When they captured a city they took all its goods and either killed the people or carried them off as captives. They were terribly cruel.

The Hebrews in Israel suffered from the Assyrians as much as everyone else, and in the Bible you can read how they were always prophesying their doom; 'And He [God] will . . . destroy Assyria; and will make Nineveh [one of the main Assyrian towns] a desolation.' It must have sounded like wishful thinking at the time.

Yet their prophecy came true. When an Englishman called Henry Layard visited Assyria in 1840 he saw only a deserted plain dotted with steep, bare hills, or mounds. These mounds, he realized, must cover the towns and villages of ancient Assyria and one of them must be Nineveh itself. Here was none of the splendour of Egypt, where statues and columns stood in still-cultivated fields. 'Assyria,' wrote Layard, was a land 'where desolation meets desolation.' Yet it fascinated him. It had more mystery than any of the other ruins which he had seen. And he had seen many, for he had been travelling around the Middle East on horseback for two years now. He and another young man had come to explore regions where few Europeans had been. They travelled alone and unarmed and were often robbed. But they came to know the people and speak their language. They learnt to avoid trouble in even the wildest places, and to get their few belongings returned to them when they were stolen. Layard was a man of strong character and gained so much influence over the Arabs that later on they even asked him to settle their family squabbles and act as their judge. He began to dream of Assyria and of coming back one day to explore the mounds: and his dream came true.

One spring morning in 1846 a great commotion arose on top of one of these mounds. A crowd of Arabs had been digging a deep hole there. Now they began to shout or pray or wave their arms. One, his eyes starting from his head, ran off as fast as he could to the nearest town. Two others jumped on their horses and galloped off to find Henry Layard. 'Hurry,' they shouted, 'for the diggers have found Nimrud himself.' This was the cause of their fear; in the bottom of their hole a giant head had emerged from the ground and stood as high as themselves. They were afraid the god was coming to life.

Layard was not at all frightened. He was delighted. When he set the men to dig on this mound he had hoped to find just such colossal statues as this. For a Frenchman, Paul-Emile Botta, had dug into another Assyrian mound at Khorsabad three years before and had found a huge palace whose door-ways were guarded by pairs of giant statues of bulls with human heads. And inside the Assyrians had gloatingly lined its walls with carved reliefs of their battles.

Layard was lucky and found two palaces on the first day he started digging on the mound called Nimrud. He dug trenches till he reached the bottom of the walls, and when he found reliefs he told his men to tunnel along beside them. This saved moving the earth above. It was very exciting, he said, going into these tunnels and seeing the strange sculptured reliefs in the semi-darkness, with bits of broken urns and other objects sticking out from the sides of the tunnel. He was really only interested in the reliefs, for the British Ambassador to Constanti-

Reconstruction of the Khorsabad Gate of the Palace of Assurnasirpal II, showing winged human-headed lions and the decorative brickwork of the period

Henry Layard at work in the desert. He and his men move the giant statues of Nimrud in the ancient manner

nople [now Istanbul], Sir Stratford Canning, who gave him the money to dig, had asked him to find them. He said they would be of interest to the people at home who, like children, enjoyed looking at pictures.

The digging was very hard work. Layard had secretly had some picks and shovels made, so that the Turkish governor of the area, who was always trying to get money from people, would not cause trouble for him. He knew the governor would think he was digging for gold and would make him pay a high price for permission to dig, if he saw him with tools. But the spades were utterly useless in the hard ground, and even the steel points of the picks were soon blunted. The workmen wielded their picks with abandon, and were more than likely to damage the reliefs with them. And of course, small objects which came beneath the picks just broke. One day when Layard saw a fine alabaster vase broken, he took the pick himself and working carefully managed to excavate whole another alabaster vase and a glass one.

He also did his best to dig out complete a horde of small ivory figures and plaques. He used his penknife for this delicate task, but the ivory was very brittle and fell to pieces as he separated it from the earth. He had no way of holding it together and he could not collect all the broken bits (though some of these were found and put together a hundred years later).

Sending the sculptures to England was another major problem. There was no good packing material in Assyria, and the Arab tribes were sometimes hostile. One load of ropes and felt sent out from England had been stolen by a tribe. Layard boldly chased them into the desert, seized the leader of the tribe and frightened him so much that he gave back the ropes. Rafts had to be made to carry the heavy stone sculptures down the river; most of the sculptures which the French had found and tried to send back to France were lost in the river when the rafts were attacked by Arab bands.

Layard made a cart to carry the giant statues and used 300 men to drag it to the river. He was amused to find a relief in the mound of Nineveh, showing the Assyrians bringing statues from the river, 2,500 years before, in just the same manner. He wanted to move as many statues as possible to England because once they were left uncovered they fell to pieces, or were broken up by Arab tribesmen who thought their religion forbade statues. He asked the British authorities to send an artist to draw the sculptures, but the authorities said they could not afford it and Layard had to do the best he could himself. As a result, some were never drawn and were lost without record.

After five years' digging Layard gave up archaeology and became a Member of Parliament. He had done the best he could with the knowledge, methods and money available. He had tried to learn about the Assyrians, draw plans of their buildings and copy all the ancient writing he found. He was followed by his assistant, Hormuzd Rassam, who was paid by the British Museum to find sculptures. He had learnt a lot, but not always the right things. Rassam was worried by competition from the French and started to excavate as many mounds as possible, all at once, to keep the French out and grab everything he could. Even where the French were already working, he tunnelled secretly by night (imagine how little his workmen could have seen, at night, in a tunnel, by candle-light). Of course he could not supervise so many digs, nor could he keep any account of what was found or where. Many Assyrian mounds were ruined by his efforts and all the information which could have been gained from them was lost.

Worse still, other people followed his example. At first the local people had thought digging for old stones was mad. They suspected the excavators were really looking for gold and when none appeared they were disappointed. But soon they learned that old stones could be turned into gold. They dug little holes all over the mounds, hacked off bits of the statues, chopped up reliefs to carry off and sell, and took away any small objects. It was very many years before the mounds were rescued from such looting.

Reading Ancient Writing

When men began to build cities and trade with other cities far away, they found it difficult to remember just how much each one should pay towards the cost of the temple or the city walls, or how much copper or wood a merchant had ordered. So writing was invented. In the valleys of the Nile and the Tigris-Euphrates rivers, a little over 5,000 years ago, men began to write their business accounts, and also to record the important things that happened to their people.

Archaeologists who found these ancient writings longed to be able to read them, for they would tell more about the past than anything else could. But people had forgotten how to read such writing long ago.

When Henry Layard discovered ancient writing carved on some of the reliefs at Nimrud, he wrote to Henry Rawlinson, British Resident (Ambassador) in Baghdad, who was studying ancient writing.

One morning in 1850, when Layard arrived at his excavations at Nimrud, he found Rawlinson lying asleep at the bottom of one of his trenches. Rawlinson was a marvellous horseman, like Layard himself, and had ridden 270 miles (435 km) to come to see the writing Layard had found.

This writing is called *cuneiform* and is the oldest known writing in the world. It looks like the footprints of small birds in a patch of mud. Men had written it for over 3,000 years in ancient times, but after that it was completely forgotten. Now scholars were trying to read it again. Henry Rawlinson was the most successful at deciphering cuneiform.

A detail of the cuneiform tablet telling the flood story

Sign of life	Sign for writing	Sign for speaking	Foreign country
Sign for abstract words	White or light	Man	Syllable ta
Syllable sha	Syllable tha	Boat	Determinative for motion

ALEPH	Y	AYIN	W	B	P
F	M	N	R	H	Ḥ
KH	H̱	S	Ś	Š	Q
K	G	T	TH	D	Z

Above: *Syllables, word signs and determinatives;* below: *the hieroglyphic alphabet*

16

He had been sent to Persia as a young soldier in 1835, and there he visited the rock cliff of Behistun where long ago a record of King Darius' rule had been carved. It was carved three times in different languages but each time in cuneiform writing. It was very difficult to reach but Rawlinson climbed up boldly and copied two of the languages.

The first used only thirty-six different signs. He found a phrase which might be the name and titles of King Darius, and starting with that he worked out the whole alphabet in two years. He could now translate the inscription, which was in Persian.

The other two languages each used hundreds of different signs. The signs represented syllables, not letters, which made them much more difficult to read. But Rawlinson knew that these other inscriptions said exactly the same as the first one, and soon he could understand some of the signs in the second language.

The third language was the one Rawlinson most wanted to read, because this was the same language that Layard was finding in the mounds of Assyria. So, in 1847, Rawlinson went back to Behistun. He met a boy from the mountains who could climb like a monkey, and the boy managed to copy the last inscription. Rawlinson immediately set to work on it. There were many hundreds of signs but in three years he had identified 150 of them and could begin to read Layard's inscriptions.

A German scholar called Oppert noticed that the writing did not fit the language they were reading. One sign could mean several sounds (just as in English 'g' sounds different in God, bridge and tough). If the writing had been invented for the language each sign would fit a sound perfectly. He guessed it had been invented for another, older language (just as our own alphabet had been). He called that language Sumerian.

Now we know he was right. The Sumerians had lived in Iraq long before the Assyrians. They built cities in the south and invented writing to keep their accounts. At first their writing was just made up of pictures, listing things owed to the temples. But by 3000 B.C. these pictures had become signs, and the Sumerians could write more complicated things.

They wrote the legends and stories of their people. Later these stories were translated by the Assyrians and others and have been found, written on clay tablets, in the King's library at Nineveh. Many thousands of tablets were found there.

One day in 1872 a young man called George Smith was translating the clay tablets in the British Museum. He found he was reading part of a story of a great flood. He was very excited because it was so like the story of Noah's Ark in the Bible. The *Daily Telegraph* newspaper offered to pay him £1,000 to go to Nineveh to look for the rest of the story. He set out knowing it would be like looking for a needle in a haystack. He had to search through all the rubbish thrown out by previous excavators but, to his surprise, on the fifth day he found the very piece of tablet he wanted. The story of Noah had come originally from a Sumerian story.

The writing of ancient Egypt, called *hieroglyphs,* was deciphered in much the same way as that of Assyria. A French soldier, who went to Egypt with Napoleon, found there a black stone inscribed with three different kinds of writing. It is called the Rosetta stone, after the place where it was found.

Scholars immediately recognized the writing at the bottom of the stone as Greek. They translated it and found that it was about King Ptolemy V. Above the Greek, the same text was carved in Egyptian everyday writing called demotic. And above that was the old Egyptian writing called hieroglyphic; this was the first form of writing that the Egyptians had invented, some time around 3000 B.C. and was used for

ceremonial texts. It is made up of small pictures of birds, animals and other objects and signs.

When the English Army defeated the French, they took away the Rosetta stone and it is now in the British Museum, but the French kept copies of it. Soon European scholars were trying to decipher the Egyptian texts. An Englishman called Thomas Young managed to work out that certain groups of signs appearing inside an oval ring, *cartouche,* referred to royal names.

In France a brilliant boy of twelve, called Jean-François Champollion,

The Rosetta Stone; a detail showing a royal cartouche and examples of all three scripts

was shown some hieroglyphs in 1802 by one of Napoleon's scholars. The boy was so fascinated that he determined to read them. He spent his schooldays studying all the languages of the Middle East, especially Coptic. Coptic is an ancient language still used in Christian Church services in Egypt, and resembles ancient Egyptian, from which it comes.

When Champollion was eighteen he started to work on the Rosetta stone. He began with kings' names, in cartouches, as Young had done, and from those he worked out the sounds of some of the signs. Then, like Rawlinson, he used the sense of the Greek text to work out some of the words in the Egyptian text; he could guess some of the ancient Egyptian words because they were like Coptic words which he knew.

All the same, hieroglyphs were terribly difficult to decipher. Champollion worked so hard on deciphering the hieroglyphs, that he literally wore himself out, and he died at the age of forty-two. But he did succeed in reading hieroglyphs: he found that some signs stand for just one letter, some stand for two or three letters, some have no sound at all, and some stand for whole words. The signs could be written from top to bottom or across, and they could run from left to right or right to left. But the animals etc. always face the beginning of the line, so you can tell which way to read them.

The Egyptians used to write on sheets of papyrus. They made these by cutting the soft inner pith of papyrus reeds into narrow strips. They placed one layer of strips one way, then another layer on top of them the other way. Then they beat them into a thin even sheet and left them to dry. In most countries such a delicate material would have rotted away, but in Egypt it has been preserved because the climate is so dry. Our word 'paper' comes from the Egyptian 'papyrus'.

Scribes wrote on the papyrus with pens made of reeds, and used black ink made of carbon or red ink made of red ochre. Many of the pen cases in which they kept their writing things have been found, as well as statues and pictures of scribes writing.

Left: Cartouches *painted on the wall of the tomb of Seti I showing the names of members of a royal family*

Below: *The Pyramids of Giza, one of the seven wonders of the ancient and modern world*

Right: *Sir Flinders Petrie (1853–1942), examining some of his pottery finds*

The Start of Scientific Excavation

Petrie, the Careful Gravedigger

William Flinders Petrie introduced the more scientific approach to archaeology. He first went to Egypt as a young man in 1880 and was to continue as an archaeologist until the age of ninety. He started at the pyramids of Giza (where we last saw Belzoni at work). There were many strange theories about these pyramids – that they represented a magic system of numbers, a horoscope for the future of mankind, a secret calendar – which Petrie wanted to test. He made very careful measurements of the pyramids and soon proved all the theories wrong. The measurements on which the theories had been based were hopelessly inaccurate.

The Pharaohs of the Fourth Dynasty had built the pyramids of Giza to be their tombs, between about 2600 and 2500 B.C. Why had they gone to the trouble and expense of building great stone mountains above their graves? It was a desperate attempt to protect their bodies. The ancient Egyptians believed they would go on to another life after death if they could preserve their bodies. So, as we have seen, they made them into mummies.

They also thought they must take with them everything they would need from this life. They filled their graves with tools, pots and pans, make-up, toys for children, and treasures for Pharaohs. And this was the problem. For the Pharaohs soon lost their treasures, and their mummies too, to thieves. So they built massive pyramids with secret entrances and passages to stop the thieves. But they were robbed. Then they built secret tombs in the Valley of the Kings at Thebes, with priests to guard them. But again all of them were robbed – all, that is, but one, as we shall see. Only the graves of the poor which contained no rich treasure, survived the robbers of the past.

Petrie was worried by the way the grave robbers and the archaeologists of his day were emptying the rich graves of ancient Egypt of any treasures left in them. They dug quickly, and with little more care than in Belzoni's time. Egypt's past was vanishing like a house on fire.

Petrie wanted to excavate in a quite different way. He wanted to learn about the history of Egypt rather than find precious objects. While working at the pyramids he thought of a way to do this. All around he saw little everyday things from the past, especially pieces of broken pottery, which archaeologists call potsherds. Cups and saucers and bowls broke all too easily then as now, but the broken pieces seem to last for ever.

Petrie saw that if he could make a complete list of all the different kinds of pottery made by the ancient Egyptians at each stage in their history, it would be the key to the past. He would be able to compare with it any potsherd he found, and know just how old his potsherd was. He would be able to tell the date of an ancient site, and how long people had lived there, just by looking at the potsherds. This was a new and important idea in Egyptian archaeology, and it is still the key to archaeological work today.

So Petrie excavated many ordinary cemeteries and ancient villages

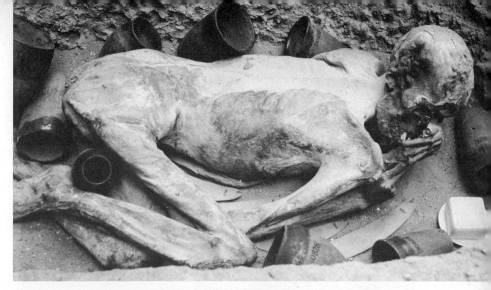

An unmummified grave of the type found at Naqada showing how the body has been preserved by the natural dryness of the climate

and towns throughout Egypt, always adding to his list of different kinds of pottery. He worked further and further back in the history of Egypt. To study the first kingdom of all he chose the cemetery at Abydos which he knew to belong to the earliest kingdoms because it had already been ransacked by another excavator. All the valuable objects had been taken away and everything else had been broken up or thrown away. But Petrie patiently collected thousands of bits of broken stone vases there. He sorted them out according to the kinds of stone. Then he spread all the pieces of one kind of stone on a long table. He picked up each piece in turn and tried to fit it together with each of the other pieces. In the end he was able to build up the shapes of 500 different kinds of vases. If a vase was found from then on with any of those shapes, he would know it came from the time of the earliest Pharaohs.

Another cemetery, Naqada, brought Petrie the most fame. He found about 2,000 graves and the people buried there lay on their sides and had not been made into mummies. They each had a collection of pots and other objects of a kind which Petrie had not seen before. He thought they might have been foreign invaders from the troubled times around 2100 B.C., when there was a lot of movement amongst the people who lived in the Middle East.

23

Examples of Prehistoric Naqada pottery;
red pictograms on natural coloured pottery,
wavy handled pottery, white crosslined pottery

He was very careful digging in this unusual cemetery. Boys looked for the patches of soft gravel, as Belzoni had, which indicated a grave. Workmen dug out the gravel until they began to see the pots. Then skilled men gently cleared away the earth from around the pots and the skeletons, and finally the most skilled men cleaned round the beads, flint knives, ivory carvings, slate palettes and other small objects. Nothing was disturbed. Petrie then listed, drew and labelled everything before it was stored away for further study.

It was this study which was so important. Petrie sorted out the Naqada pottery into pots of different kinds. There were brown pots with black tops, pots with criss-cross white lines, pots with pictures, and many pots with distinctive wavy handles. He noticed that any one kind of pot was not always made in the same way: its style had changed over the years. He could see that the style became simpler and less fine with time.

To discover the order in which the pots were made he looked to see if every kind of pot had been found with every other kind, in some grave or another. He noticed that criss-cross white-lined pots were rarely found with wavy-handled pots, and when they were it was the latest criss-cross pots with the earliest of the wavy handles. So he knew the criss-cross pots came from the earliest days of his cemetery and the wavy handles from the later times. He gave them numbers called Sequence Dates, because he did not know their real dates (criss-cross pots were thirty-one to thirty-four, wavy handles were forty onwards); then he fitted the other pots into the Sequence according to whether they were found in graves with criss-cross pots, or with early or late wavy handles. When pots similar to those with his highest numbers (seventy-seven to eighty) were found in graves from the time of the earliest kings, he realized that the cemetery at Naqada was extremely ancient, older than anything else then known in Egypt. It was used before 3100 B.C.

Petrie was the first archaeologist to excavate really carefully in the Middle East, and to report immediately everything which he found. He showed that a great deal could be learnt from broken pottery and everyday objects and that no object should be thrown away as worthless. He drew up guidelines for archaeologists to follow which enabled them to rescue the history as well as the treasures of the past. 'Most people think of excavating as a pleasing sort of holiday amusement,' he wrote reproachfully, 'but it takes about as much care and management as any other business.'

A Royal Family of 3,300 Years Ago

Tell el Amarna was one of the ancient cities excavated by Flinders Petrie. A very strange place it was too, and it was a strange story of a strange family which Petrie began to piece together there.

Other ancient Egyptian cities are marked by ruins, or have grown into modern towns. But at Tell el Amarna there was little to be seen. Traces of the city had vanished from the narrow bay of land between the Nile river and the desert hills. But the people of the poor villages in that little plain knew that if they dug in the sand they would find *sabakh*. This was a kind of mud they used to fertilize their fields. They probably did not know that it was actually the remains of mud-brick walls, thousands of years old.

One day, in 1887, a peasant woman digging for *sabakh* found hundreds of little clay tablets with odd marks on them. She had never seen anything like them. (Can you guess what they were? Of course. Clay tablets with cuneiform writing.) She sold them to another villager for about 30p. He loaded them in sacks on his donkey and set off to sell them to dealers. When he opened the sacks many of the tablets had crumbled to dust. And the dealers said the others were fakes, so many of those were soon lost too.

French and English experts heard of the tablets and some museums eventually bought them. They guessed they might be very important; and so they were. They were letters sent to a Pharaoh called Akhenaten from the princes and rulers of his empire to the east. They told of quarrels and struggles in the Middle East around 1360 B.C. and many asked the Pharaoh to send help, or soldiers, or gold.

Model of a house at Tell el Amarna, showing the internal structure

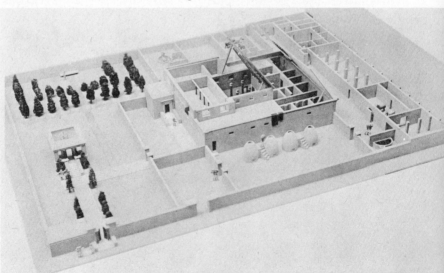

A drawing from a relief, showing the Pharaoh Akhenaten and his family distributing necklaces as rewards to their ministers

In 1891 Petrie came to dig where the tablets had been found. He discovered the outlines of a great palace and fine streets and work shops where beautiful glass and *faience* (glazed vases, tiles, beads, etc.) had been made. And he could see from bumps in the ground that a large town had once stood there.

But all the buildings had been knocked down and only the bottom of the walls still stood: beneath these walls was nothing but desert sand. There had been no town at Tell el Amarna before the one he was excavating, and no town there ever after. And yet the palace which he found there had been very splendid, a royal palace. It had painted and tiled walls and floors and beautiful decorations. The artists of Tell el Amarna must have been among the finest of ancient Egypt.

The puzzle of Tell el Amarna fascinated archaeologists and many others followed Petrie. In 1905 N. de Garis Davies copied the pictures on the walls of the tombs which were cut in the rock cliffs behind the town. They were unused and damaged but they were decorated with magnificent paintings and reliefs showing the royal family giving presents, driving through the streets, receiving visitors, or simply enjoying life at home or in their gardens. Never had pictures such as these, showing the private life of a Pharaoh (in one he was actually kissing his wife), been found in Egypt.

A German, Ludwig Borchardt, excavated at Tell el Amarna from 1904 to 1914. He found the studio of the palace sculptor, Thutmose. In it were the models and masks from which the sculptor carved the heads of the royal family. About twenty carved heads, some of them unfinished, were lying there too. The most famous of these is a painted limestone head of Queen Nefertiti.

English archaeologists dug there from 1921 to 1937. One of the first of them, Leonard Woolley, excavated the grand house of Nekht, the king's minister. Among its many rooms was a large reception hall with columns. And the main bedrooms each had a private bathroom and earth-closet lavatory. Woolley also found a small royal palace and pleasure garden to the south of the town. It had a boating lake, flower beds marked still by patches of mud and the roots of trees and shrubs, and kennels with masses of greyhound bones.

The workmen became very skilled at revealing even traces of brick dust and paintings from wooden doors, using their wide-bladed hoes. British archaeologists, led later by John Pendlebury, were able to trace many of the buildings in the town. They could match some of these foundations with the pictures in the tombs and so were able to make models of the town as it once was.

The Story of the Royal Family

These excavations enabled archaeologists to work out much that had happened at Tell el Amarna. They found, from inscriptions and boundary stones, that it was built by the Pharaoh Amenophis IV around 1370 B.C. This Pharaoh forbade the worship of all the old gods of Egypt and told his people to worship only the sun disk, called the Aten. He changed his own name to Akhenaten, meaning 'in the service of the Aten'. He wanted a new capital for his new religion so he built the city at Tell el Amarna, half way between Cairo and Thebes, and called it Akhetaten, meaning 'the horizon of the Aten'.

A broad Egyptian collar of faience beads

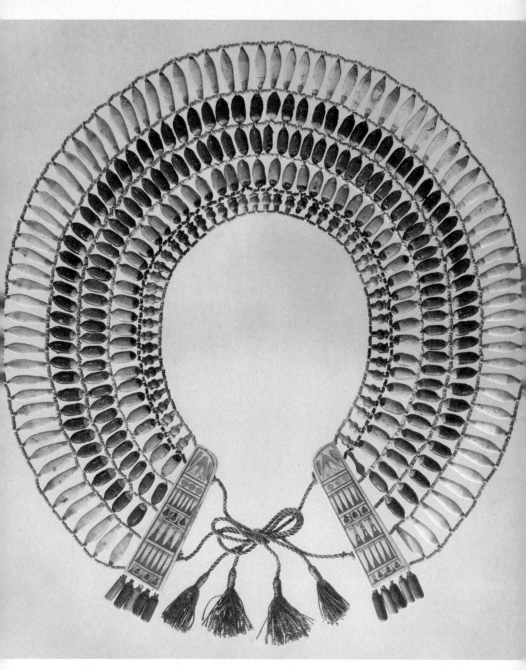

Akhenaten had a beautiful wife, called Nefertiti, and six daughters, but no sons are shown in the paintings. The oldest daughter, Meritaten, married a prince called Smenkhkare, who ruled with Akhenaten for the last few years of the latter's life. But Smenkhkare died young. The second daughter died while still a child, and the third daughter Ankhe-senpa-aten married a boy called Tutankhaten, later changed to Tutankhamun.

Tutankhamun ruled for about nine years after Akhenaten's death, then he, too, died when he was only about eighteen. During his rule old advisers made him change back to the worship of the old gods and move his capital back to Thebes. Some years after his death, the town at Tell el Amarna, which had stood for only about twenty-five years, was deliberately destroyed. Akhenaten's face was hacked off any picture and sculpture where it was found.

Tutankhamun's teenage widow knew, if she married again, that her husband would be Pharaoh, and she was afraid that an old adviser called Ay, old enough to be her grandfather, would marry her. She wrote to the King of the Hittites, a great rival nation in the north, asking for one of his sons as a husband. Her letters have been found at Boghazköy, the Hittite capital in Turkey. But the prince delayed in setting out, and then was murdered on the way. Ay probably married Ankhesenpa-aten as he did become Pharaoh, and her name has been found linked with his in the royal cartouche on a ring. Nothing more is known of her.

We seem to know so much about the private lives of this family and yet much remains a mystery. Who, for instance, were Smenkhkare and Tutankhamun? Pharaohs usually married their sisters, but Akhenaten's daughters apparently had no brothers to marry. The exciting discovery of the tomb of Tutankhamun in the Valley of the Kings at Thebes made the problem all the more interesting. The tomb was found in 1922 by Howard Carter who first went to dig with Petrie at Tell el Amarna when he was a boy of seventeen. Then he dug for years in the Valley of the Kings, always searching for this one lost tomb. At last he found it, almost intact, with an incredible treasure inside it.

Tutankhamun's mummy has been examined and x-rayed by doctors who found he died at the age of eighteen or nineteen, possibly from a

The Treasury Room of Tutankhamun's tomb, showing the many treasures that accompanied the Pharaoh in death

blow on the head. Another mummy, found in 1907 in the tomb of Akhenaten's mother, Queen Tiy, was examined by R. G. Harrison, Professor of Anatomy at Liverpool, in 1963. He found the bones were of a young man of about twenty (one of the wisdom teeth was not cut and many bones which fuse together in an adult had not yet done so). By now people suspected that this was Smenkhkare. Harrison asked a medical artist to build up a face to fit the skull, without telling him where the skull came from. The face he drew looked very like that of Tutankhamun! The skeletons are so alike that they must have been close relatives, probably brothers or half-brothers – perhaps sons of Akhenaten's father.

In Tutankhamun's tomb were also the mummies of two babies, born dead. They were probably his children, the last members of the ill-fated family of Akhenaten.

Left: *A painted statuette of Nefertiti and Akhenaten*

The frieze of the two princesses, showing two of the daughters of Akhenaten and Nefertiti

Ur of the Chaldees

Leonard Woolley left Tell el Amarna in Egypt in 1922, and went to dig in Iraq. He chose to excavate there the mound of Ur of the Chaldees, famed as the home of Abraham in the Bible, but of which nothing else was known.

The southern part of Iraq is dotted with the mounds of ancient cities, just like Assyria in the north. These southern cities had flourished long before those of the Assyrians. They had been built originally from about 5000 B.C. onwards and from about 3000 to 2000 B.C. they were the towns of the Sumerians, the people whom Oppert had recognized as the the inventors of cuneiform writing. But excavating these ancient city mounds had not been at all easy. The Sumerians had built with mud brick, because they had no stone, and the early excavators did not know how to excavate mud brick walls, so could not find any buildings in the mounds. Also, the south country was wild and dangerous, which made it hard to concentrate on archaeology. One early excavator was attacked every night by lions who ate all his guard dogs. Then he had to leave in a hurry because of floods. The first Americans to excavate there also had to leave in a hurry when they were attacked by wild tribesmen and their camp was destroyed.

When Woolley started to dig, life was more peaceful and there were no more lions. He had the advantage of knowing the careful excavating techniques developed by Petrie, and he also knew how to excavate mud brick walls. German archaeologists who had dug at the mound of Babylon from 1898 had discovered how it should be done. They scraped the surface of the ground until stripes of a darker earth appeared. These were the walls. Then they dug out the earth to make a trench a little way away from the side of the wall. Finally they very carefully flaked off the mud sticking to the face of the wall. In this way they were able to dig out all the mud brick buildings of the great city of Babylon. And Woolley was able to dig out the houses and temples of Ur.

Ur had lasted a long time as a city and it had had its ups and downs. One of the 'downs' was when it was captured and destroyed by King Samsu-iluna of Babylon, in about 1737 B.C. The houses were all destroyed and many of their owners' belongings were buried in them. It was not very pleasant for the owners of the houses but it was a gift for Woolley.

The lower part of the walls of all the houses had survived, so Woolley could uncover the plan of a whole district. He worked out that the houses were two storeys high, because in some of the richer homes he found the bottom steps of brick staircases leading upwards. The houses were built round an open courtyard and in them he found charred wood where a post might have supported a balcony above. Behind the house was another small courtyard with a vault in which those who died were buried. But the many small children who died were buried in big jars under the family chapel.

The district was going downhill before it was destroyed, and several large houses had been turned into business offices. Woolley was puzzled by one house. Here the doors between the rooms and the courtyard had been blocked up and a new door made from the yard to the street. He found about 2,000 clay tablets here. They included multiplication tables, history lessons, practice writings and so on. They showed that the owner of the house, Igmil-sin, had turned it into a school.

Many of the clay tablets which Woolley found had not been baked but only dried in the sun. They were as soft as the mud around them and almost impossible to dig out of it. Early excavators had not even noticed such soft tablets. Woolley found the only thing to do was to dig out a lump of earth with the tablet in it, put the lump in the oven and bake it like a cake. This made the tablet hard and the earth could be brushed off.

One year Woolley decided to dig a deep pit right through the mound of Ur to uncover the different cities which had been built there, one above another. After each foot or so of earth he found different kinds of pottery and other objects, and as he dug lower down the pottery he found was older than that above. He was able to make a list, like Petrie's, of the pottery from each period of the history of Ur. Woolley dug until he reached pure mud with no pottery in it. He had not expected to reach the bottom of the mound at this point, so he carried on digging. He dug through eight feet (2·4 m) of mud, then he came to pottery again, the pottery of the people who built the first town of Ur. The mud was silt from a great flood which had drowned their town. Woolley thought it must have been Noah's flood, described in the Bible. But the same great layer of silt was not found in other ancient towns near by, so perhaps it was just a local flood.

The most important building, even for the early inhabitants of the city, was their temple. There they worshipped their gods, and soon the temple came to own much of the land. The Sumerians never destroyed their temples; when they wanted a new one they covered the old with earth and built on top of it. After a while the temple stood on a platform. Then they began to build high pyramids (with the old temples still buried inside them) and the new temples on top. These were called ziggurats. Ur-Nammu, King of Ur from about 2113 to 2096 B.C., built a huge ziggurat which still stands today, 4,000 years later. It is rather ruined but Woolley was able to work out from what was left how it must once have looked.

When Woolley started to dig at Ur he came across a place where many gold beads were found. Quickly he stopped digging there. He did

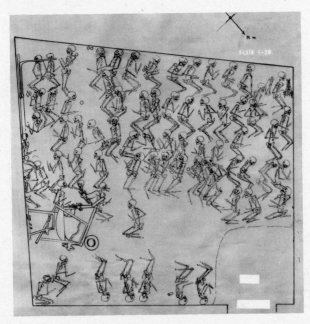

Woolley's drawing of the pit of Ur, showing the unexcavated harp and skeletons

not know enough about Ur to tell how old the beads were (he guessed wrongly by 1,600 years), and he was worried because his workmen were tempted to pocket the gold. He decided to wait.

Four years later, when he knew the city and the workmen, he went back to the 'gold trench'. He found the beads came from a cemetery, and this time he dated it correctly to 2300 B.C. Beneath the cemetery were many older graves, and among them sixteen very strange ones. The graves, he thought, of kings and queens. A sloping ramp had been dug down to these graves. It led to a room behind which was the tomb of the king or queen. At the foot of the first ramp lay five skeletons of soldiers with copper daggers. In the room behind lay the skeletons of ten women, in neat rows, and at the end of the rows was a magnificent harp, with the harpist lying dead across it. Then came a wooden chariot with the skeletons of the asses that had pulled it, and the grooms who had driven it. Gold glittered everywhere and all the ladies wore magnificent headdresses of gold, lapis lazuli and carnelian.

In the other tombs Woolley found similar scenes of death. In one eighty-four skeletons lay peacefully. Among them was a girl whose silver hair ribbon was found coiled up in her pocket. She must have been late dressing for her own funeral and had not had time to put it on. Woolley worked out that when a king died the men and women of his court went down into the tomb where soothing music was played to them. They all drank from the small cups he found and then they went to sleep; never to wake again.

Among the skeletons were many beautiful and extremely fragile ornaments in gold and mosaic. Most were crushed flat. Woolley cleaned them with a small knife and soft brush. Then he poured paraffin wax over them and bound it with a wax cloth. When it set he removed the whole lump. By warming it he could soften the wax enough to press the

The harp of Ur after reconstruction

treasures back into shape. He recovered a harp, of which the wooden frame had rotted away, by pouring liquid plaster into the holes in the ground left by the wood. When the plaster set he was able to dig out the complete shape of the harp.

Woolley's rescue of the treasures of Ur was a brilliant job. It was only possible because of the methods introduced by Petrie. In Layard's day such treasures would have fallen to pieces in the excavator's hands.

Archaeology Today

In recent years archaeology has become far more complicated, and an excavation will take months to prepare. The leader must collect a team of archaeologists each of whom can do some specialist task.

At the site one man will be in charge of surveying (measuring) the ground and drawing a plan of it. He will have a long black-and-white ranging pole and various instruments (plane table, plumb bob, telescopic alidade, T-square, spirit level, etc.) for measuring heights, distances and angles. He will also mark out the areas to be excavated.

When objects are found one of the team will photograph them, another will draw them and another record them. There may be an architect to work out the plans of buildings and a conservator to preserve fragile or crumbling objects. All the team will help with the work of excavating. To start with workmen remove the top soil with picks and shovels and carry it away in baskets. Some excavations now use a mechanical digger or small railway to remove large amounts of earth. As soon as objects are found the archaeologists must work more carefully, scraping with little pointed trowels, using a hard brush to clean the surface of the ground (which will show the outlines of objects, buildings or ditches), and a soft brush to remove soil from delicate objects.

They will have a collection of labelled boxes and bags into which they will put their 'finds', and some plastic bags in which they seal up objects to be sent to laboratories for testing. The following chapters tell of archaeology today in the Middle East, where modern machinery and new scientific discoveries are making a great deal of difference.

The Oldest Town in the World

A city much older than Ur of the Chaldees was excavated in the 1950s. It is called Jericho, and like Ur is famous because of a story in the Bible.

The Bible tells that when the Israelites came to invade the Holy Land they had to capture Jericho first, an impossible task. Then God told their leader, Joshua, to march round the walls of the city for seven days, and on the seventh day seven priests should blow on seven horns. Then the walls of the city would fall flat.

Several archaeologists had tried to find out more about this strange story by digging at Jericho. In 1952, Dame Kathleen Kenyon, decided that it would be worth excavating there again, because more was now known about the different kinds of pottery found there.

The mound of Jericho is very steep and very high. She dug a trench from top to bottom of the slope of the mound. And she found ring after ring of ancient city walls. It needed very careful excavation to find out how old the various walls were. Miss Kenyon employed very few work-men to dig out the earth, and a large number of archaeologists to watch for changes in the layers of earth and pottery, and to work out which wall belonged to which layer.

They found that all the walls in the mound of Jericho had been built before the time of Joshua. There were no walls at all from Joshua's day. Could they have been carried away by the heavy rains which washed away the top of the mound? Or could the story of Joshua have been mixed up with the story of some earlier attack on Jericho, made by other Israelites? Archaeology has not yet been able to answer those questions.

But if this huge mound had been built up before 1300 B.C., when could the first town have been built at Jericho? Miss Kenyon found that the town with the first city walls had been built by people who lived so long ago that they had not even known how to make pottery. They had built round houses of mud brick and a massive stone tower, nearly thirty feet (9·1 m) across, for defence. The tower has a flight of stairs going up inside, and still stands thirty feet (9·1 m) high today. Joined to it was a city wall over six feet (2·1 m) thick, also of stone. But finally this town was abandoned, we do not know why. After a while other people came to Jericho. They built another town with square houses, and new walls of their own, but they still had not learnt to make pottery.

Under the floors of their houses were found skulls, with faces made of plaster and eyes of shells. And there were very many skeletons with no heads under the same floors. The people of the town must have collected the skulls of members of their family who died, and made faces for them with plaster.

Miss Kenyon sent the objects she found in these ancient towns to various laboratories where scientists examined them. She found a few grains of wheat and barley in the oldest town. These were examined and found to be of a kind grown by man, not wild grain, so the people must have known how to farm the land. She found many animal bones from the same period, but they were larger than the usual farm animals and must have been wild ones. The people of the town seem to have hunted for their meat, and may not have learnt to keep their own flocks.

Now Miss Kenyon wanted to find out how old this town was. None of the ways of discovering the age of things which we have seen so far was any help. But in 1946 a new scientific method of telling the age of things had been developed. It is called Carbon-14 dating.

Scientists know that the radioactivity in the atmosphere causes all living things, plants and animals, to absorb Carbon-14 atoms while they are alive. When they die this Carbon-14 disappears very, very slowly. They know how many Carbon-14 atoms a tree or an animal has when it dies, and how long it takes to lose them. When an archaeologist brings them a piece of ancient wood or bone they measure how many Carbon-14 atoms are left in it, and calculate how long it has been dead to within a hundred years or so. And for archaeologists this is very useful.

Miss Kenyon found some burnt wood in the oldest town at Jericho. She sent it to different laboratories to be examined. The answers which came back were amazing. The wood was about 10,000 years old. So Jericho was first built in about 8000 B.C. and is the oldest town we know of in the world.

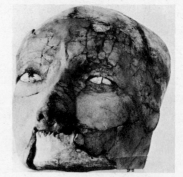

Plastered skull from Jericho

Science and Pottery Fakes

The scientist handed back the pottery bowl to the man from the museum. 'I am afraid your bowl is no more than twenty years old,' he said. The man from the museum looked slightly downcast. His museum had recently bought this bowl in London, and it had cost a great deal of money. It was said to come from a place called Hacilar in Turkey and was supposed to be about 7,500 years old. Now he knew that it was a fake, made in the last few years, and worth nothing.

The story of Hacilar is a fascinating one; and that is why museums and collectors were prepared to pay high prices for pottery found there. The low mound at Hacilar was discovered by a British archaeologist, James Mellaart, in 1956 when he was walking in Turkey, looking for archaeological sites. The following year he began to excavate the mound. He found the place was very ancient indeed. The first village, in the lowest level of the mound, was shown by Carbon-14 dating to have been built in about 7000 B.C. It was not quite as old as the earliest town of Jericho, but nearly.

In fact it was rather like the second town of Jericho, where the people buried skulls beneath their floors. Here, too, Mellaart found human skulls, propped up on stones and buried beneath the floors. And in this earliest village, also, the people had not known how to make pottery.

Then for many years no one lived in the village. This was shown by the fact that the tops of the house walls had crumbled away, and been washed over the site in a thin, greenish-yellow layer. But people returned to Hacilar in about 5750 B.C. and by then they knew how to make attractive pottery. Soon they were making fine little clay statues, too. These statues were of girls or women and the tallest of them was only ten inches (255 mm) high. They were probably of a goddess whom people worshipped.

This town was burnt down but another was built in its place and the people were still making strange figures of a goddess. These were now hollow pots (a little like a piggy bank), with one head or two heads, and a creamy colour with red stripes. The heads had eyes made of obsidian (a hard shiny stone) but no mouths.

After four years, Mellaart left Hacilar and the Turkish authorities helped him fill in his excavations with a bulldozer, so that people should not dig there for loot. Looting of ancient objects is still a problem in the Middle East, and in Turkey, a huge country with hundreds of ancient sites in remote and lonely places, it is very difficult to stop it. The Turkish government has strict laws against smuggling antiquities out of the country, but as long as people abroad pay high prices for them, the smugglers will stay in business. A few years after Mellaart left Hacilar, pottery and figures like those he had found appeared for sale in Europe and America. Museums and private collectors paid hundreds of pounds for these strange and ancient objects. A museum in Oxford bought one of the hollow pots with two heads. It looked splendid, but when they examined it very carefully they began to doubt its authenticity. Somehow it was not the same as the pieces which Mellaart had given them (he gave all the complete pots he found to a Turkish museum).

The museum took their pot to the Research Laboratory for Archaeology in Oxford. Scientists at the laboratory were just developing a new method for telling the age of pottery. They called it *thermoluminescence testing*. *Thermo* means heat and *luminescence* means light. The scientists found that when they heated ancient pots to 350°C or more, the pottery glowed with a faint light. This is because radioactivity in the clay, soil and atmosphere causes light to collect in pottery over a very long time. By measuring the amount of light that comes from a pot when it is heated, the scientists can calculate roughly how old that pot is. But pottery which has been made recently, and baked at a high heat to make it set hard, gives off no light. All the light in the clay has been cooked out, and there has not been time for more to collect.

The scientists found that of sixty-six pots and figurines which they tested, only eighteen gave out light. They were genuine ancient pots. The other forty-eight gave off no light and were modern fakes.

People had started to dig at Hacilar soon after Mellaart left. They had been lucky and found quite a few complete pots; they had, of course, found out nothing at all about the history of the site because they were only digging for pots. But even this was hard work. They might dig for days and find nothing. So they began to make copies of ancient pots themselves. And without the thermoluminescence tests their fakes might never have been proved.

The Animal Mummies of Saqqara

Archaeologists have recently been excavating a cemetery at Saqqara which was used by the ancient Egyptians for over 3,000 years. Early Pharaohs and their courtiers were buried there. The first pyramid was built there. It is called the Step Pyramid and was designed for Pharaoh Djoser by his extraordinary architect and 'prime minister', Imhotep. It made Imhotep so famous that later he was considered a god.

Professor Emery was in charge of the excavations at Saqqara until his death in 1971. He was examining the tombs of the ancient courtiers when he found that the shafts leading down to their graves were cut across by large tunnels, about twelve feet high by eight feet wide. And they were stacked from floor to ceiling with the mummies of birds; in one set of tunnels were ibis birds, in another falcons. Leading off these tunnels were others filled with the mummies of baboons and in a separate tunnel were cows. Funeral stones told that the cows were buried there in the last 300 years before Christ. Each baboon was seated behind a stone door on which its name was written, where it came from, when it was brought to live in the temple, and a prayer for its eternal welfare. For these were no ordinary animals and birds. They were sacred ones which represented Egyptian gods, and their bodies had been preserved as carefully as those of the ancient Egyptians themselves. They were treated with palm wine, salt (natron), frankincense and myrrh, oils and resins. Then they were bandaged with the limbs and wings beside the body, so some of them looked like a long sausage with a head on top. On some of the ibises the bandages were carefully wound into a pattern and a picture of a god was fixed on the front.

Animal gods had always been worshipped in ancient Egypt. When the first Pharaoh took over the whole country in about 3100 B.C. he brought many different tribes under his rule. The tribes had animals as sacred mascots and these animals were absorbed into the Egyptian collection of gods. Many Egyptian gods were given an animal form: they could be drawn either as human beings, or as ordinary animals, or very often as humans with animal heads.

The falcon represented one of the most important gods called Horus.

He was the special god of the Pharaoh, who was himself thought of as a god as well as a king. The ibis and baboon represented Thoth, the god of writing. They also represented a more recent god, Imhotep, the architect of the Step Pyramid because he was wise like Thoth. This may be why so many of them were found at Saqqara, near the foot of his pyramid. The cow represented the goddess Isis, mother of Horus and wife of the great god of the dead, Osiris.

Osiris himself was linked with the bull. Tunnels full of mummies of sacred bulls had been found at Saqqara a hundred years ago, by a Frenchman called Mariette. Mariette knew nothing of those tunnels when he went to Saqqara in 1850, but he did notice the head of a sphinx sticking out of the sand there. He remembered the story of a Greek called Strabo who visited Saqqara at about the time of Christ. Strabo described seeing the sacred bull led out of the temple to be worshipped by the people. And he told of an avenue of sphinxes leading to the tombs of previous sacred bulls. Mariette followed the line of sphinxes and found tunnels full of gigantic stone coffins. In a chapel at the entrance to the tunnels, he found a statue of a sacred bull, and was surprised when some local women clambered on its back and sat there silently for a moment. He was told they were women who had no children but now they hoped to be able to have some. So the sacred bull had not quite lost its magic appeal.

Left: *The animal mummies of Saggara*
Rescue work at the great temple at Abu Simbel

Rescuing a Temple

At the beginning of this book we saw that giant of a man, Belzoni, discovering the great temple at Abu Simbel in southern Egypt. He dug away the sand which buried it, in the hope of finding statues and columns which he could send back to England. But he was not lucky. The temple was hollowed out of the cliff, and its statues were carved in the living rock and could not be moved.

It was a colossal and very beautiful temple. The rock from which it was carved was pink and red, and glowed in the rays of the rising sun. The temple faced east and, as the sun rose across the River Nile, it shone in through the doorway. It lit up the faces of the statues of the gods in the innermost room, right inside the cliff.

For 150 years people came to visit and admire the great temple of Abu Simbel, and the smaller one near by. But recently a new danger threatened the temple. It was going to be buried again, this time by water, not sand, and the water would destroy it. A great dam was being built across the Nile, and above the dam the water would rise in a huge lake, drowning the temples of Abu Simbel and many other ancient buildings as well. The dam was completed in 1964 and gradually the river below the temples began to rise up its banks.

The Egyptians were very upset that they were going to lose their ancient buildings. They asked the United Nations Educational, Scientific and Cultural Organization (called Unesco for short) to help them. Unesco asked countries all round the world to give money to help save the temples, and ideas of how to do it. It would be very difficult to move these temples because they were hollowed out inside the rock.

Many plans were sent to Unesco. Some suggested that the temples should be surrounded by a dam to keep the water away. But they would have stood in a kind of pit in the middle of the lake, and the rising sun would never again shine on the faces of the gods. Also the water might still seep in and damage them. Another plan suggested enclosing the temples each in a giant concrete box and cranking them up with jacks, as you jack up a car to change the wheel. But this would have been terribly expensive.

At last Unesco chose a plan proposed by Sweden. It planned to cut the temples up into large blocks and carry them to the top of the cliff, and then to build a new cliff there with the temples inside it, to look just as they did before. The job would be done by a group of five countries working together.

In 1964 the temples were surrounded by the strangest scene which had ever come before them in all the years that they had stood there. Bulldozers crept up and down the slopes of sand, giant cranes waved their arms in the sky, saws like huge cheese saws moved backwards and forwards, scaffolding rose all round, concrete mixers churned all day, and scientists probed and tapped. The scientists had to make sure that when the temples were cut into blocks they would not break up or crumble away. They had to repair any cracks or weak places in the rock, and strengthen the most crumbly parts by injecting synthetic resin into them.

Meanwhile Unesco collected money and counted the cost. Governments, organizations, individual people, even children in schools, collected for the temples and gave millions of pounds. It cost £14,000,000 to save the temples. About 150,000 tons of rock had to be moved. But now the two great temples of Abu Simbel stand once more above the Nile, facing the rising sun. They are probably the most expensive temples in the world, and saved thanks to people from all round the world. To each country which contri-buted the Egyptians gave a valuable ancient object.

Archaeology in the Middle East has come a long way in the 150 years since Belzoni strode alone through the ruins of ancient Egypt, carrying off anything he could move.

The famous carved figures of Abu Simbel

Chart of Events and People Mentioned in the Book

from 10000 B.C.	Men learn to farm the land in the Middle East. They move down into the river valleys.
from 8000 B.C.	Villages are built. At Jericho there is a fortified town. At Hacilar the first town is built.
from 6000 B.C.	Men begin to make pottery. They also learn to use metal but their tools are still usually of stone.

	IRAQ (Sumer and Assyria)	EGYPT
4000 to 3000 B.C.	Cities are built in Sumer. Each one is head of a small state and ruled by a king or governor. Writing is invented.	Cemetery of Naqada is in use. Writing is invented. The King of Southern Egypt conquers the north and makes Egypt one land, about 3100 B.C.
3000 to 2000 B.C.	Sumerians at the height of their power. Royal graves of Ur c.2650. Ziggurat built at Ur c.2100.	Cemetery of Abydos c.3100–2700. Pyramids: c.2660 Imhotep builds Step Pyramid for Pharaoh Djoser. Courtiers' cemetery at Saqqara. Pyramids of Giza c.2600–2500.
2000 to 1000 B.C.	End of Sumerian power. Babylon becomes the most important city. Ur captured by King Samsu-iluna of Babylon c.1737. Assyrians begin to be important, for short periods at a time.	Tell el Amarna built by Pharaoh Akenaten (1379–1362). Tutankhamun (1361–1352) moves capital back to Thebes. Great conquerors, the Pharaohs Seti I (1318–1304) and his son Ramesses II (1304–1237) extend Egyptian empire. Temples of Abu Simbel built.
1000 B.C. to 1 A.D.	Assyria becomes strongest state. Nimrud founded as capital by Assurnasirpal (884–859). Khorsabad founded as capital by Sargon II (721–705). Assyrian empire includes Holy Land. Assurbanipal (668–631) founds library at Nineveh. Invades Egypt 661. Assyria conquered by Medes from Persia 612. Babylon conquered by Persians 539.	Animal cemeteries built at Saqqara, especially after 500. Egypt invaded by Assyrians (671–661). Egypt conquered by Persians (525).

Both lands were ruled by foreigners from then on. Iraq became a poor province but the Egyptian civilization survived for hundreds of years more.